Titles in this series:
The World's Greatest Business Cartoons
The World's Greatest Cat Cartoons
The World's Greatest Computer Cartoons
The World's Greatest Dad Cartoons
The World's Greatest D.I.Y. Cartoons
The World's Greatest Golf Cartoons
The World's Greatest Keep Fit Cartoons
The World's Greatest Marriage Cartoons
The World's Greatest Middle Age Cartoons
The World's Greatest Rugby Cartoons
The World's Greatest Sex Cartoons

Published simultaneously in 1993 by Exley Publications in Great Britain and Exley Giftbooks in the USA.

12 11 10 9 8 7 6 5 4 3

Selection © Exley Publications Ltd.
The copyright for each cartoon remains with the cartoonist.

ISBN 1-85015-441-4

Front cover illustration by Roland Fiddy.
Edited by Mark Bryant.
Printed and bound in Malta.

Exley Publications Ltd, 16 Chalk Hill, Watford, Herts WD1 4BN, UK.
Exley Giftbooks, 232 Madison Avenue, Suite 1206, NY 10016, USA.

Cartoons by Langdon, Mahood, Schwadron and Smilby reproduced by kind permission of *Punch*. Cartoons by Heath reproduced by kind permission of *Spectator*. Pages 32 and 33 © Rich Tennant/® The 5th Wave, Humor + Technology, Rockport, MA, USA.

THANK YOU

We would like to thank all the cartoonists who submitted entries for *The World's Greatest COMPUTER CARTOONS*. They came in from many parts of the world – including Greece, New Zealand, Holland, Canada, the United Kingdom, Northern Ireland and the USA.

Special thanks go to the cartoonists whose work appears in the final book. They include Enzo Apicella page 38; Mike Atkinson page 21; David Austin page 39; Les Barton pages 20, 41, 58; Hector Breeze page 50; Hugh Burnett page 69; Martha Campbell page 6; Clive Collins pages 46, 59; Stidley Easel pages 49, 51; Roland Fiddy cover, title page and pages 5, 14, 15, 23, 48, 66, 70, 71, 72, 73, 76; Toni Goffe pages, 7, 26, 27, 29, 74; Michael Heath page 68; Martin Honeysett pages 11, 12, 13, 16, 17, 24, 30, 31, 34, 35, 36, 37, 63; Tony Husband pages 42, 43, 44, 45, 52, 54, 55, 62, 75; David Langdon page 28; Larry pages 8, 47, 56, 57, 64, 65, 67; Kenneth Mahood page 40; David Myers pages 60, 61; Viv Quillin page 25; Harley Schwadron page 9; Smilby page 22; Bill Stott pages 4, 10, 18, 19, 53, 77, 78, 79; Rich Tennant pages 32, 33.

Every effort has been made to trace the copyright holders of cartoons in this book. However, any error will gladly be corrected by the publisher for future printings.

THE WORLD'S GREATEST

COMPUTER

Cartoons

EDITED BY

Mark Bryant

EXLEY

NEW YORK • WATFORD, UK

"And this is a more analytical analysis of the analysis
you analyzed last week."

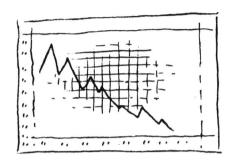

"If Adam and Eve had an Apple, why did they have so much trouble accessing God's instructions?"

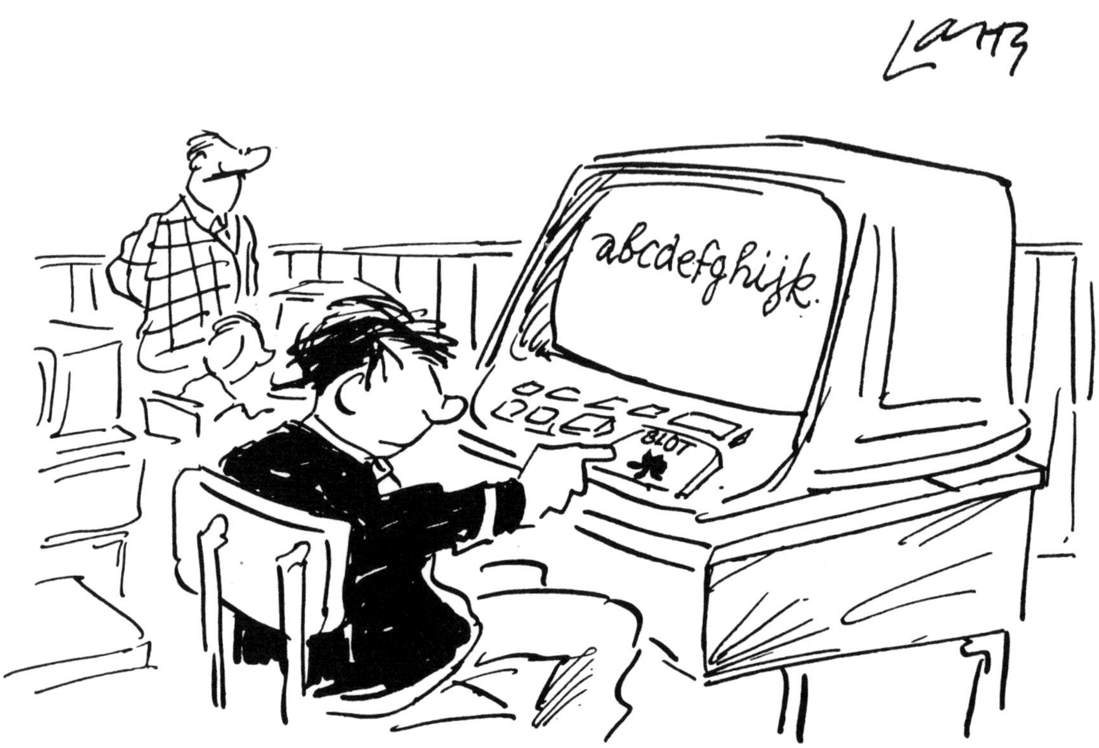
abcdefghijk.
SLOT
Larry

"This year I have quite a long and complicated list.
Are you computer-accessible?"

"Just think — at the push of a button I can send 300 tons of Andalusian lemons speeding to the market places of north-west Belgium!"

"We fed the ingredients of the new food into the computer
and these are the brand names it's come up with."

11

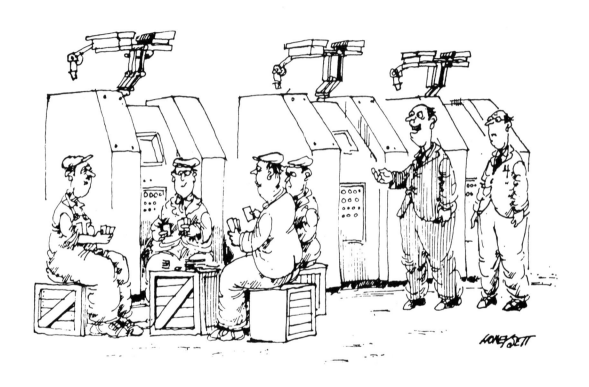

"With this new computerized machinery
we can have more of our men playing cards than ever before."

"He's just made another five million profit.
Now he wants to find out who sells the cheapest champagne."

13

DON'T YOU KNOW THAT GIRLS ARE NO GOOD ON COMPUTERS ?!
Congratulations! You have reached Level 5

"I fed all your symptoms into the computer,
Mr Bilkins, and it died."

"All right, you lot, which one of you programmed a dead rat onto Miss Pringle's computer?"

17

"I asked her if she thought her new V.D.U. was pretty..."

"Don't you want to play anymore, Daddy?"

*"According to my computer, we missed a real bargain
in the Bahamas this week!"*

"Computer Snow Vacations...?"

"Hello — I think I'm onto something."

The computer fanatic knows that computers are INFALLIBLE...
...it is the Human Factor that messes things up.

23

"This is the one we use to send out final demands."

27

"I see. You failed mathematics, but you can hack into the
US National Security Agency."

29

"And I bought this one to explain the manual of the first one."

"Harry likes to know exactly how poor we are."

"Alright, steady everyone. Margo, go over to Tom's PC and press 'ESCAPE', . . . very carefully."

"Oh yeah, and try not to enter the wrong password."

"They've arrested him for the computer fraud and the computer as an accessory."

"The computer tells us when the brew has reached the required concentration."

35

"I'm all for computers, they do all the dull, boring jobs for you."

"It says it's the Student Union picket line and the
strike committee are over at the Duke's Head."

IN CASE OF FAILURE

"The Government has hacked into his computer and asked for ideas to solve the deficit!"

"He's left the computer to the cat."

"Can she call you back? She's nearly defeated
'Zorg the Invader from Hell'."

"My name is Carole, and I play up to 20 computer games a day."

"No, Sir, that's its IQ. The price ticket is on the right hand side..."

IT'S QUITE SIMPLE, DAD — EACH COMMAND IS IDENTIFIED BY ONE OR MORE LEADING KEYWORDS, AND MAY HAVE A NUMBER OF PARAMETERS, SOME OF WHICH ARE OPTIONAL. EACH PARAMETER MAY BE AN EXPRESSION INVOLVING CONSONANTS, VARIABLES AND FUNCTIONS....

BREAK GLASS
IN EMERGENCY

Easel

49

"I suppose one day I'll get round to replacing the whole thing by a silicon chip."

"Look, I'd best be going home now otherwise my home computer
will be getting suspicious."

"You'd best go — he'll be finished on the computer soon
and he'll notice you."

"Computers are just like men. Punch the right buttons and they're all yours…"

"Sex is O.K., but we prefer to play on the computer these days."

"Oh please don't leave me Julia... how will I get on without you?"

"He was a computer error of the Computer Dating Service!"

"Perhaps we should take Benton off computers for a spell."

"And this, Sir, is our most advanced model…"

".... The meaning of Life, hang on, I'll check with the computer."

"*Even with the fully automated assembly line,
we've still got some of the old problems.*"

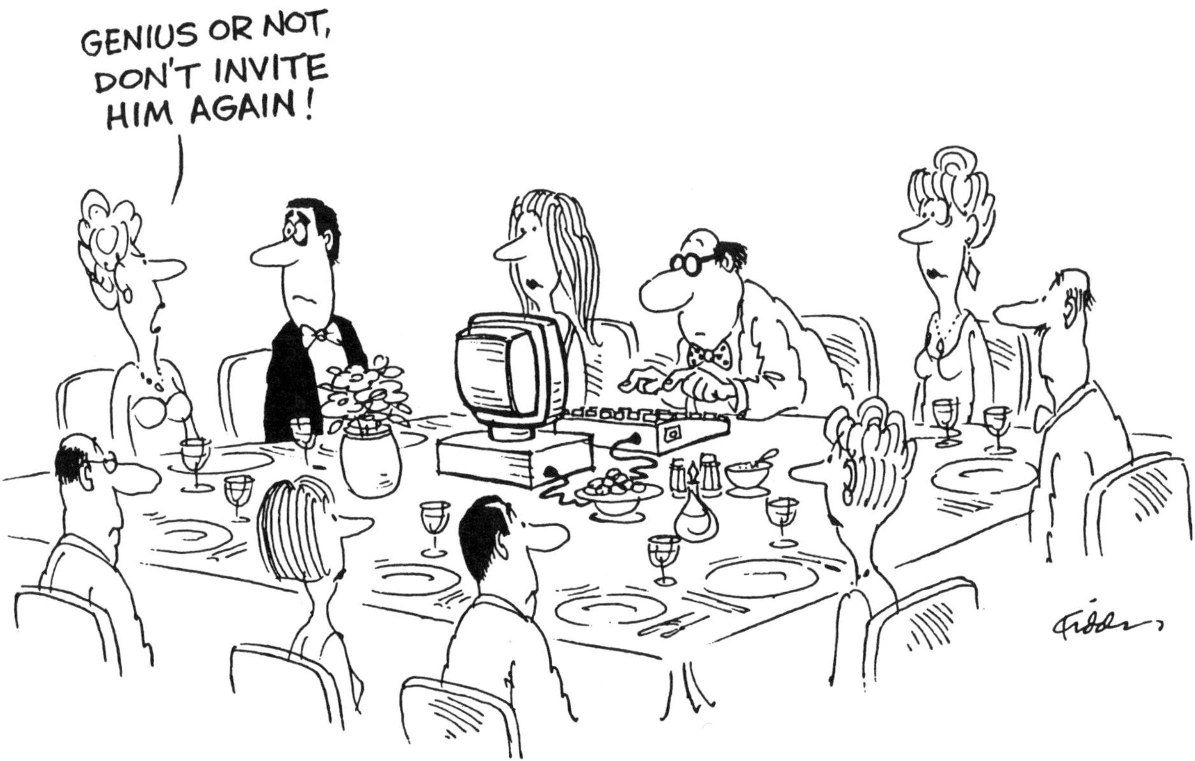
GENIUS OR NOT, DON'T INVITE HIM AGAIN!

The computer fanatic is a serious person — some might say obsessional.

"Miss Thompson, find out if the office computer system
takes Ninja Killer computer games."

"You're right, the fault you reported is basic.
It's called 'not-plugged-in'."

1. "O.K. I need the bottom line on net profit next year."

2. "What's that weird 'beep beep'?"

3. *"That's the closest a MKII A/K 9334/4 gets to sardonic laughter..."*

Books in "The World's Greatest" series
($4.99 £2.50 paperback)

The World's Greatest Business Cartoons
The World's Greatest Cat Cartoons
The World's Greatest Computer Cartoons
The World's Greatest Dad Cartoons
The World's Greatest Do-It-Yourself Cartoons
The World's Greatest Golf Cartoons
The World's Greatest Keep Fit Cartoons
The World's Greatest Marriage Cartoons
The World's Greatest Middle Age Cartoons
The World's Greatest Rugby Cartoons
The World's Greatest Sex Cartoons

Books in the "Victim's Guide" series
($4.99 £2.50 paperback)

Award-winning cartoonist Roland Fiddy sees the funny side to life's phobias, nightmares and catastrophes.

The Victim's Guide to Air Travel
The Victim's Guide to The Baby
The Victim's Guide to The Boss
The Victim's Guide to Christmas
The Victim's Guide to The Dentist
The Victim's Guide to The Doctor
The Victim's Guide to Middle Age

Books in the "Crazy World" series
($4.99 £2.50 paperback)

The Crazy World of Aerobics
The Crazy World of Hospitals
The Crazy World of The Office
The Crazy World of Sailing
The Crazy World of School

The following titles in this series are available in paperback and also in a full colour mini hardback edition ($6.99 £3.99)

The Crazy World of Bowls
The Crazy World of Cats
The Crazy World of Football
The Crazy World of Gardening
The Crazy World of Golf
The Crazy World of Housework
The Crazy World of Marriage
The Crazy World of Rugby
The Crazy World of Sex

Books in the "Fanatic's Guide" series
($4.99 £2.50 paperback)

The **Fanatic's Guides** are perfect presents for everyone with a hobby that has got out of hand. Eighty pages of hilarious black and white cartoons by Roland Fiddy.

The Fanatic's Guide to Dogs
The Fanatic's Guide to Money
The Fanatic's Guide to Sports

The following titles in this series are available in paperback and also in a full colour mini hardback edition ($6.99 £3.99)

The Fanatic's Guide to Cats
The Fanatic's Guide to Computers
The Fanatic's Guide to Dads
The Fanatic's Guide to D.I.Y.
The Fanatic's Guide to Golf
The Fanatic's Guide to Husbands
The Fanatic's Guide to Love
The Fanatic's Guide to Sex